First published by Scribble, an imprint of Scribe Publications, 2019
This edition published in North America in 2020. Reprinted 2020
18–20 Edward Street, Brunswick, Victoria 3056, Australia
2 John Street, Clerkenwell, London, WC1N 2ES, United Kingdom
3754 Pleasant Ave, Suite 100, Minneapolis, Minnesota 55409 USA

Text © Eun-ju Kim 2017
Illustrations © Ji-won Lee 2017
Consultant: Jong-oh Kim

Originally published in Korean as 쏠까, 말까? 플라스틱
by Woongjin Thinkbig Co., Ltd, 2017
Translation © Joungmin Lee Comfort 2019
This edition was published by arrangement with the S. B. Rights Agency.
Printed and bound in China by 1010

FSC
www.fsc.org
MIX
Paper from
responsible sources
FSC® C016973

Australian hardback 9781925849196
UK hardback 9781912854134
UK paperback 9781912854325
North American hardback 9781950354061

CiP records for this title are available from the National Library
of Australia and the British Library

scribblekidsbooks.com

Plastic

past, present, and future

TEXT BY
EUN-JU KIM

ILLUSTRATION BY
JI-WON LEE

S

SCRIBBLE

On the night of January 10, 1992, a fierce storm
raged through the western Pacific Ocean.
As gigantic waves pummeled a large cargo ship,
stacks of shipping containers fell overboard
and tumbled into the churning sea.

When the containers burst open, thousands
of plastic bath toys came out, turning the swirling
sea into an enormous bathtub. It was on that
day the plastic ducks, turtles, beavers, and frogs
began a long and unusual journey.

About ten months after the accident, dozens of plastic bath toys began to appear on the beaches of Alaska. The toys had bobbed thousands of miles across the Pacific Ocean.

Although some of the toys had lost their brilliant colors in the harsh sun and seawater, they were still nearly as perfect as bath toys could be. The toys continued to wash up along the western coast of the USA for a long time.

In fact, the wayfaring toys showed up on various shores around the world. Some went up north and got trapped in the Arctic ice. Some others continued to travel in the Atlantic Ocean and made their way as far as Scotland.

But even at the end of their long adventures, the toys still looked almost as good as new. How did they stay so fresh?

The tough little toys were made out of plastic.
And because plastic is light and durable, the toys
could travel far with the currents and the wind
while holding their shape against the rough waves.

What would have happened if the toys had been
made out of a different material?

If made out of wood, they would have turned brittle
from the seawater and crumbled into pieces.

If made out of glass, they might have shattered while tumbling out of the shipping containers.

If made out of metal, they would have sunk to the bottom of the sea and rusted away.

Bath toys are just one of the countless things made out of plastic. Look around you now and you'll see plastic products everywhere. In fact, it is impossible to go a day without stumbling across something made out of plastic.

How about we take a walk through this house and look for plastic products?

Toys

Computer keyboard and monitor

Pillow stuffing

Bed sheets

Bowls

Plastic bags

Cups

Sauce bottle

Milk jug

Plates

Counter top

Apron

Seat cushion

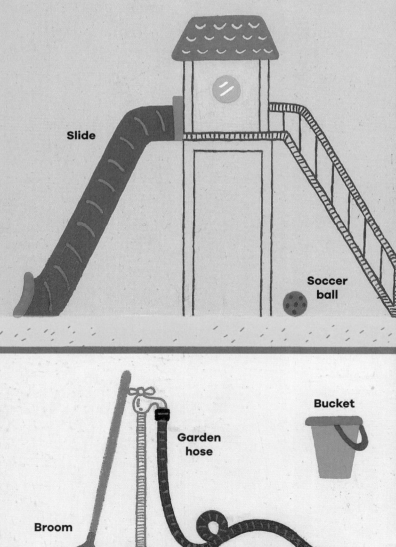

Slide

Soccer ball

Bucket

Garden hose

Broom

Shampoo bottles

Towels

Bath toys

Soap dish

Toothbrushes and toothpaste tube

Shower curtain

Bath cap

Shower head

Bath stool

Spatula handle

Picture frames

Pot handle

Chopping board

Refrigerator handle

Planter

Helmet

Handlebars

Elbow pads

Bike seat

Pedals

Tires

Bike path

Why do you think there are so many
things made of plastic?

It's because plastic can be easily molded into
any shape. Plastic becomes soft with heat. Then pressure
is applied to mold it into the desired shape. As the
plastic cools, it hardens in the shape it was molded.
In this way, factories manufacture a massive variety
of plastic goods every day.

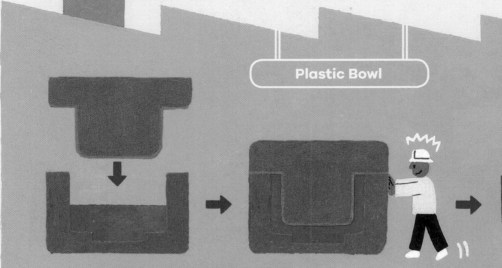

Plastic Bowl

Molten plastic is poured into a mold
and then pressed into desired shape.

When the plastic cools,
the mold is removed.

Plastic Toy Duck

Molten plastic is sprayed into a mold. Air is blown into the mold,
forcing the molten plastic against the inner walls of the mold.

When the plastic cools,
the mold is removed.

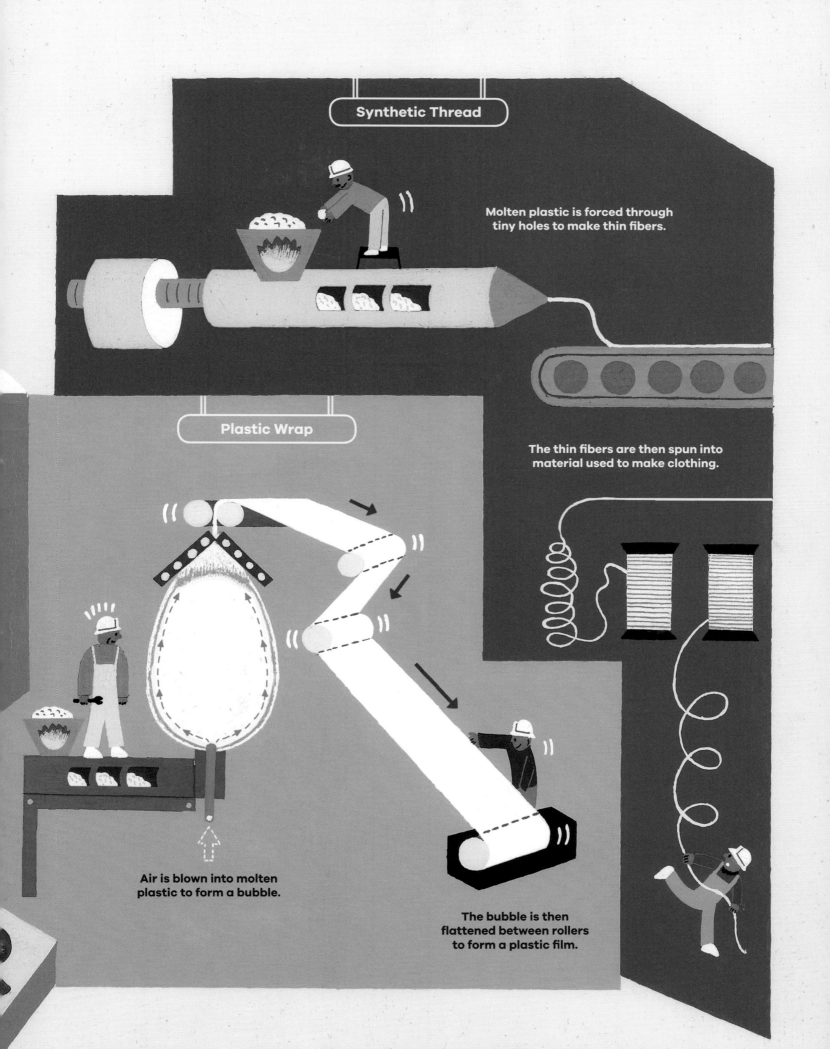

Synthetic Thread

Molten plastic is forced through tiny holes to make thin fibers.

The thin fibers are then spun into material used to make clothing.

Plastic Wrap

Air is blown into molten plastic to form a bubble.

The bubble is then flattened between rollers to form a plastic film.

Most plastics are made from petroleum.

Naphtha, a substance extracted from petroleum, is used to create various types of plastics. Each plastic's unique properties and characteristics determine what kind of finished products may be manufactured with it. Things like frying-pan handles are made with heat-resistant plastic. Things such as squeezable sauce bottles are made with flexible plastic.

Oil

As petroleum is heated, it separates into different components.

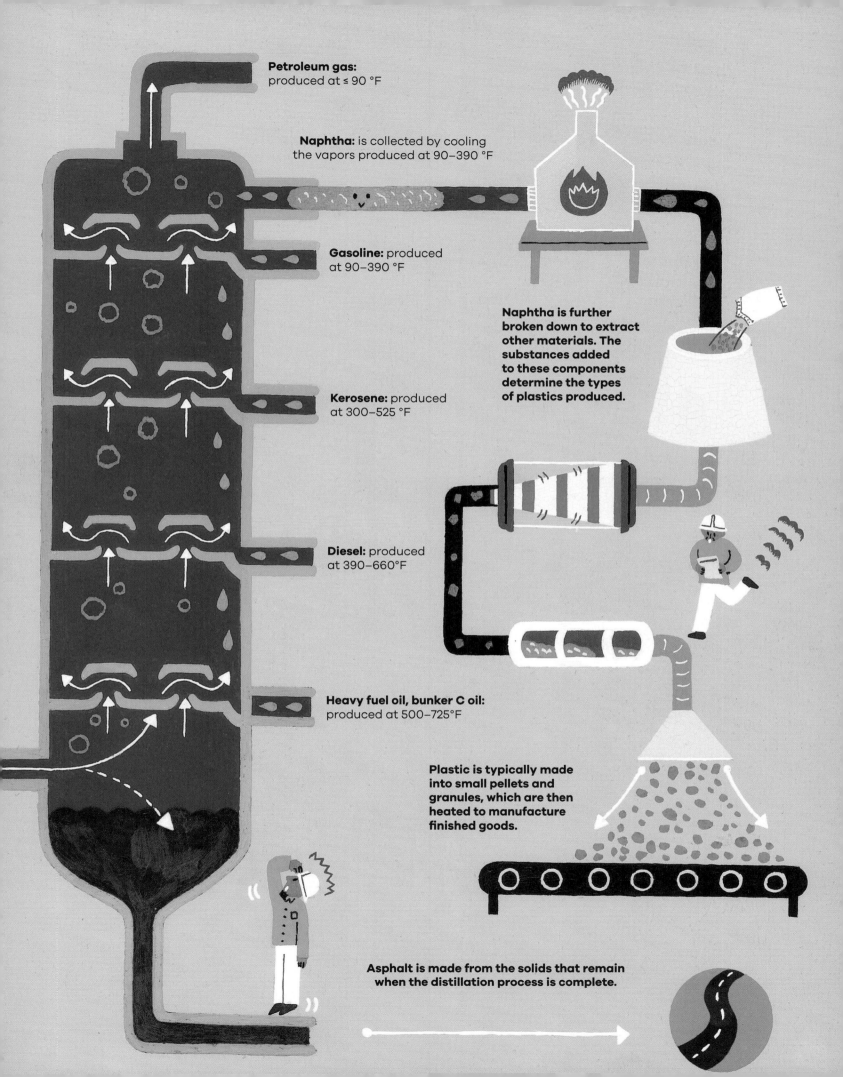

Petroleum gas: produced at ≤ 90 °F

Naphtha: is collected by cooling the vapors produced at 90–390 °F

Gasoline: produced at 90–390 °F

Kerosene: produced at 300–525 °F

Naphtha is further broken down to extract other materials. The substances added to these components determine the types of plastics produced.

Diesel: produced at 390–660°F

Heavy fuel oil, bunker C oil: produced at 500–725°F

Plastic is typically made into small pellets and granules, which are then heated to manufacture finished goods.

Asphalt is made from the solids that remain when the distillation process is complete.

Supermarkets are bursting with products packaged in plastic.

Because plastic is light and tough, plastic packaging makes it easier to transport these products.

Let's compare two 2L bottles, one made of plastic and the other made of glass.

A 2L plastic bottle weighs about 1.5oz. A 2L glass bottle weighs over 50oz.

Not only does the plastic bottle weigh far less than the glass bottle, it is also far less likely to break.

Due to plastics, today's cars are lighter than those that used to be manufactured with steel parts. Airplanes and rocket ships also weigh less because of plastics.

Lighter weight means less fuel is needed to travel the same distance.

In this way, plastics help us to conserve energy.

Plastic has also improved the safety and quality of healthcare for us.

How so? Well, before disposable plastic syringes were introduced, glass syringes had to be sterilized and then reused again and again. But improperly sterilized syringes often spread dangerous diseases between people.

Today's plastic syringes are designed for one-time use only, which eliminates such risks. Disposable gloves, medicine bags, and tubes are some of the many plastic products used in medicine today.

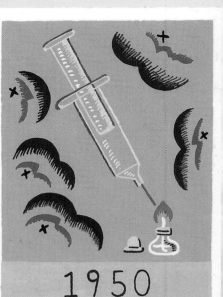

1950

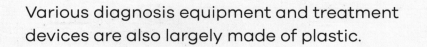

Various diagnosis equipment and treatment devices are also largely made of plastic.

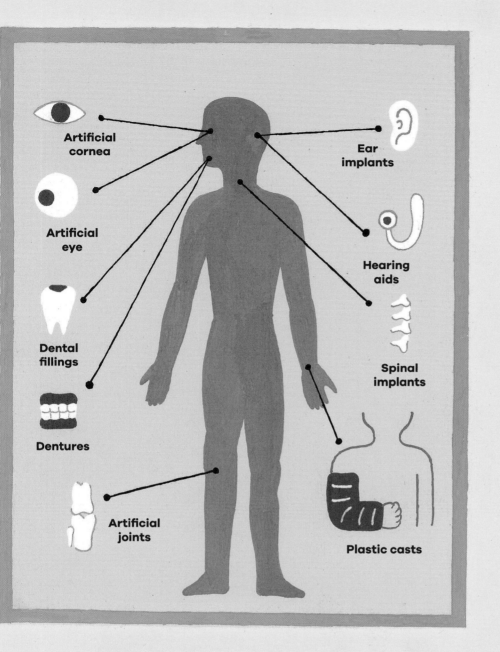

Artificial
cornea

Ear
implants

Artificial
eye

Hearing
aids

Dental
fillings

Spinal
implants

Dentures

Artificial
joints

Plastic casts

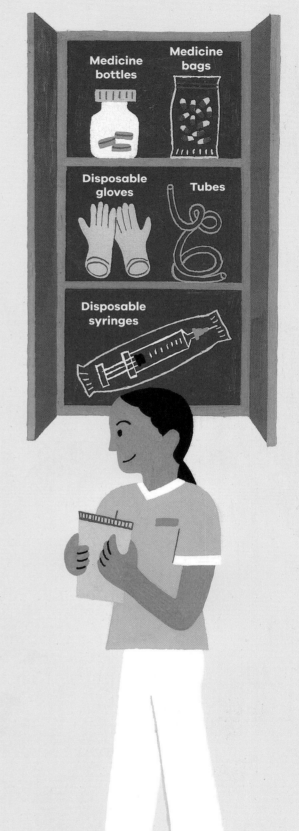

Medicine
bottles

Medicine
bags

Disposable
gloves

Tubes

Disposable
syringes

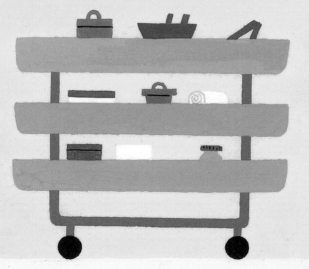

What do you think? Do plastics help us to stay healthy?

So, when did we start using plastic?

In the late 1860s, the first plastic, called celluloid, was invented while people were searching for an alternative material for billiard balls. Back then, billiard balls were made with ivory, which was very expensive.

In 1907, a new petroleum-based plastic called Bakelite was invented.

From then on, various types of plastics were steadily introduced, including nylon and PET. And because plastic proved cheap and easy to produce, it quickly came to replace natural materials such as wood, glass, stone, metal, rubber, cotton, and silk — in addition to ivory.

1869

CELLULOID, THE NEW WONDROUS MATERIAL, SAVES THE ELEPHANTS.

1938

NEWSPAPER

So long silk hosiery. Nylon hosiery is here to stay! Meet the miracle fiber so thin, yet tough as steel.

1948

PLASTICWARE PUSHES GLASSWARE OUT OF THE KITCHEN. LIGHTER AND MORE AFFORDABLE THAN GLASS!

Plastic

1973

Say hello to plastic bottles. Lightweight and shatterproof!

Factories began churning out a wide variety of plastic products in staggering quantities. Goods that used to be expensive became easily affordable to most people. As a result, plastic use jumped to more than twenty times what it had been fifty years before.

Today, the world consumes over 300 million metric tons of plastic each year, which include as many as 1 trillion plastic bags. That comes out to about 2 million bags per minute.

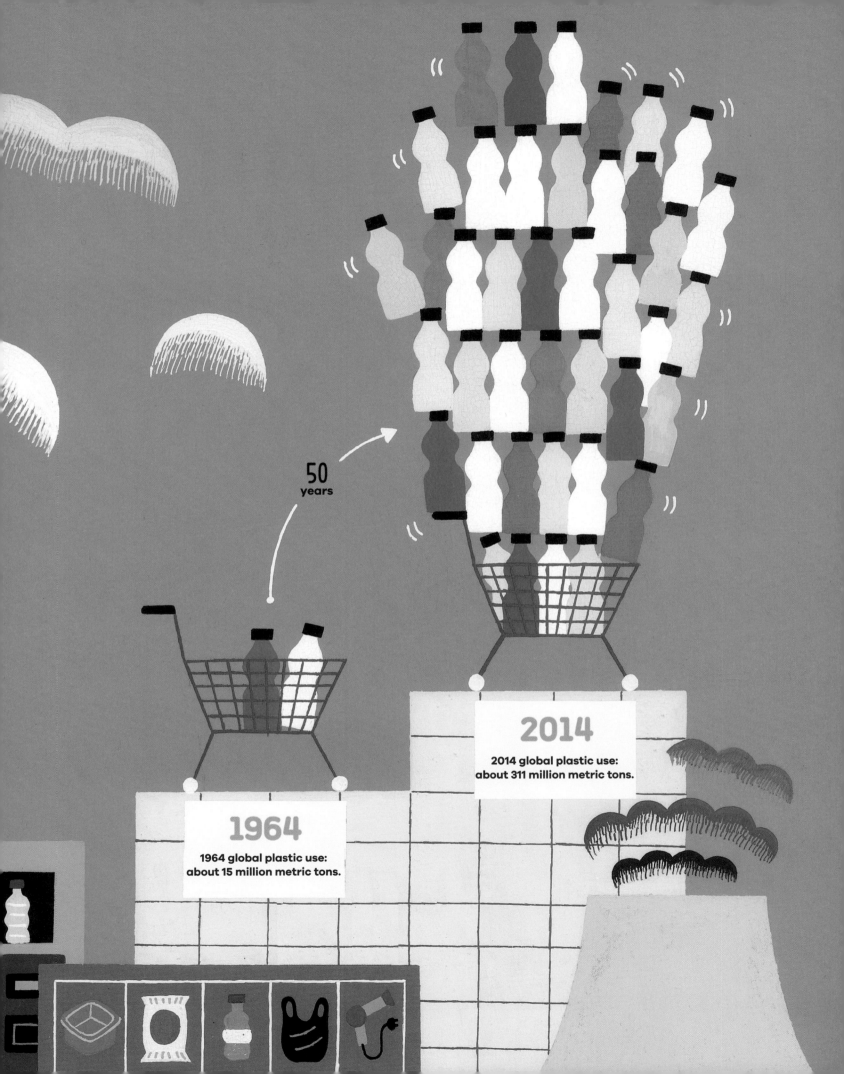

50 years

2014

2014 global plastic use:
about 311 million metric tons.

1964

1964 global plastic use:
about 15 million metric tons.

Just as our plastic use has become enormous, so has the amount of plastic waste we've come to generate.

Every year, the world produces about 28 million metric tons of plastic waste.

Where does it all go?

A small portion of it gets recycled, but the majority simply gets burned or buried in landfills. Burning plastic releases toxins that pollute the air and harm the health of animals and plants. Some toxins are even known to cause cancers in the human body.

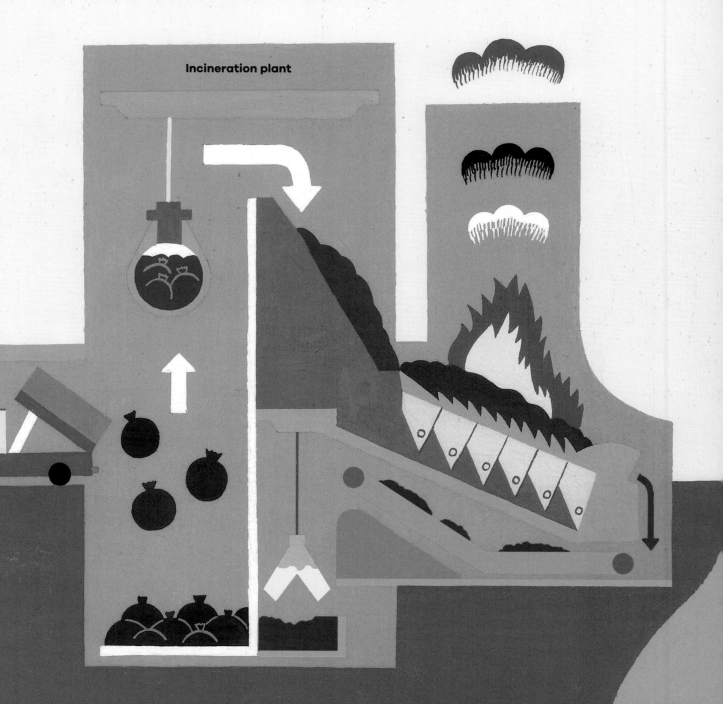

Incineration plant

Ordinary trash dumped in landfills typically breaks down naturally over time. But plastic can take hundreds of years to biodegrade.

Durability, a very useful quality of plastic, is also contributing to a huge environmental problem.

Landfill

Paper:
2–5 months

Cotton:
1 year

Leather:
25–50 years

Metal:
over 100 years

Plastic:
hundreds of years

Over 8 million metric tons of plastic waste
enters the ocean each year.

As water travels on land, it picks up and carries with
it all kinds of plastic junk into the sea. Once plastic waste
reaches the sea, it keeps traveling the world's oceans with the
wind and the currents, just like the bath toys did.

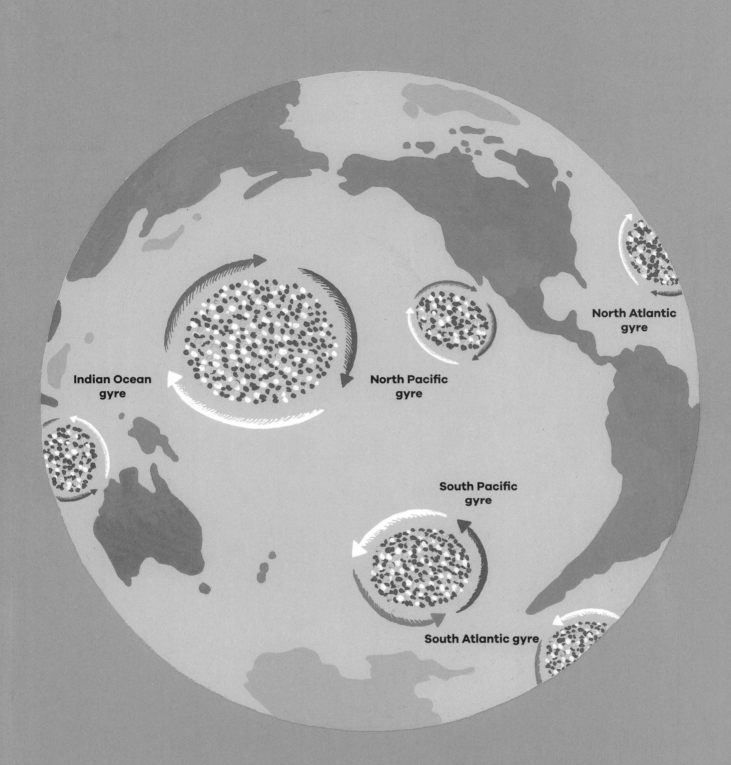

Plastic waste adrift at sea tends to accumulate in patches where ocean waters swirl in movements known as gyres.

All kinds of plastic debris swirl about in these patches, including plastic bottles, plastic bags, toothbrushes, bottle caps, toys, fishing lines, fishing nets, etc. These giant patches of rubbish are found throughout the world's oceans. The one floating in the Pacific Ocean today is larger than Great Britain and is known as the 'Great Pacific Garbage Patch'.

Plastic pollution has a devastating effect on sea animals.

Sea turtles eat plastic bags, mistaking them for jellyfish, and slowly starve to death. Sea lions become tangled and injured in abandoned fishing gear, which often leads to the animals' deaths.

Adult albatrosses confuse plastic debris for food and feed it to their chicks. As the chicks' stomachs fill with plastic, they slowly die.

Fish also ingest plastic fragments that damage their health.

Where do these plastic fragments come from?
Over time, a lot of the plastic trash floating in the ocean breaks down into smaller pieces because of the waves and sunlight. Some of these pieces of plastic are the size of birdseed. Others are so small that they are barely visible without a microscope.

These tiny plastic fragments are called microplastics.

How are sea creatures affected by water polluted with microplastics? Like magnets, microplastics attract harmful substances in the surrounding water. As animals swallow these plastics, toxins accumulate in their bodies and poison them. In particular, young fish who fed on microplastics were found to swim more slowly and have stunted growth.

What can we do about plastic pollution?

The most obvious solution is to reduce our own plastic use in the first place — even if it's inconvenient. In Rwanda, single-use plastic bags have been made illegal. Shoppers use reusable paper bags and cloth bags instead. At airports, visitors from other countries are required to turn in any single-use plastic bags they've traveled with.

Arrivals

SECURITY

San Francisco banned the sale of bottled water in schools and other public areas to reduce the amount of plastic waste the city generates. Instead, water fountains have been installed all across the city.

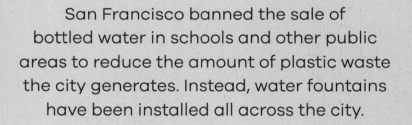

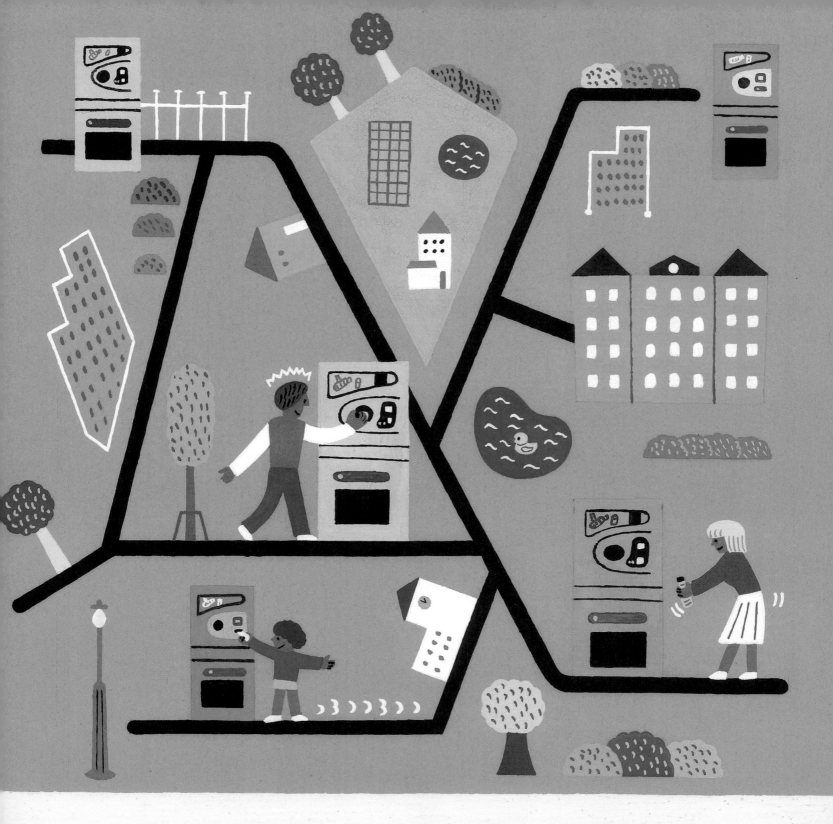

If we can't avoid plastics, then we must use
them responsibly, through reuse and recycling.

In Denmark, there are reverse vending machines everywhere
to encourage recycling. Citizens deposit empty bottles in these machines,
and the machines spit out cash in return. Introduction of these machines
has allowed Denmark to recycle most of its plastic bottles.

Plastic waste can be recycled and molded into all kinds of new and useful plastic products. Like this, recycling helps to conserve petroleum, the raw material for plastic. It also helps to reduce the amount of plastic waste that ends up being burned or dumped in landfills.

1. Plastic waste is collected.

01 PET

06 PS

05 PP

03 PVC

2. Collected waste is sorted by type.

3. Sorted waste is then compressed into bales and sent to recycling facilities.

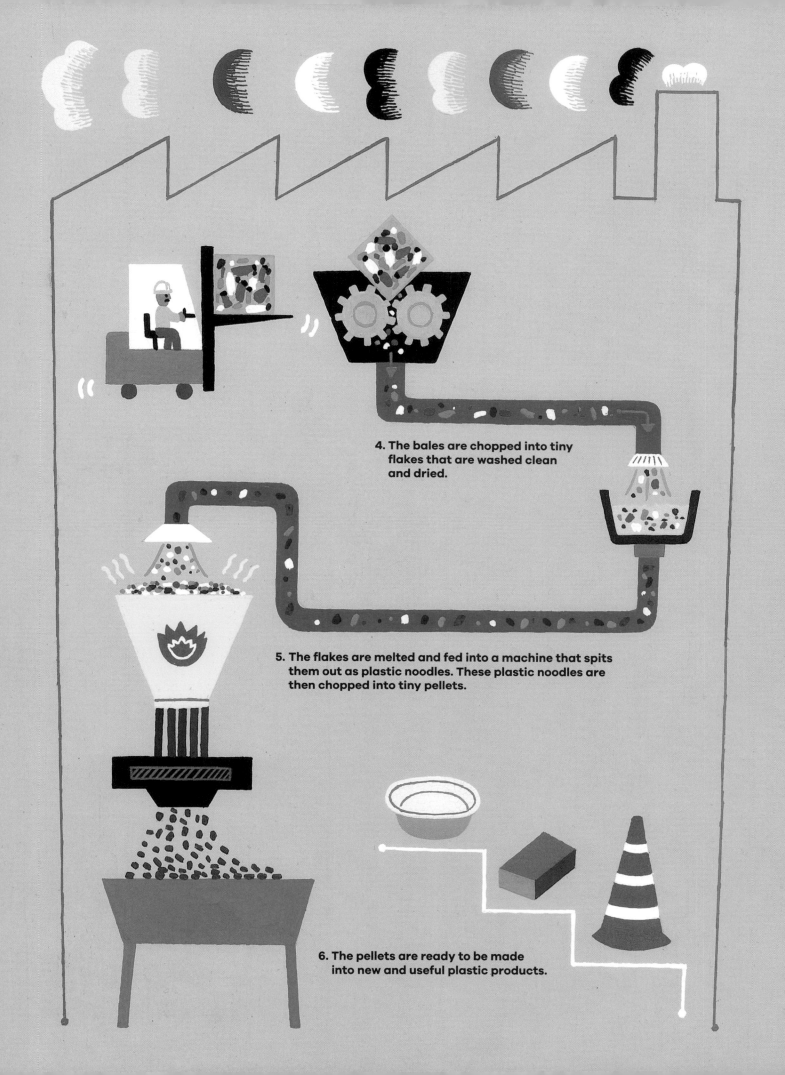

4. The bales are chopped into tiny flakes that are washed clean and dried.

5. The flakes are melted and fed into a machine that spits them out as plastic noodles. These plastic noodles are then chopped into tiny pellets.

6. The pellets are ready to be made into new and useful plastic products.

Unfortunately, recycling alone cannot solve our plastic problem.

Some plastic items cannot be recycled at all. Plus, the same piece of plastic can only be recycled so many times before it becomes useless, as the quality decreases with each recycling. Recycling plastic also requires a lot of time and money. Many people, especially scientists, are continuing to look for new ways to solve these problems.

Scientists have been researching biodegradable plastic and other ways to help bacteria to break down plastic in the environment.

Some companies convert plastic waste back to oil. In this way, they turn troublesome trash into a resource.

In 2010, the *Plastiki*, a boat made out of 12,500 plastic bottles, completed a journey across the Pacific to raise awareness about the widespread problem of plastic pollution.

A 19-year-old inventor, Boyan Slat, introduced a new way to clean up our oceans. His ocean plastic clean-up system, a U-shaped floating barrier with a long skirt attached below, is designed to catch plastic debris swirling in the currents.

Plastics have helped to improve our lives in many ways.

But they also pose a serious threat to the environment.

What can you and I do to use plastics more responsibly?

Visit our website
for additional resources
and ideas about what we
can do to reduce global
plastic waste:

scribblekidsbooks.com/books/plastic/